THE HOW AND WHY WONDER® BOOK OF
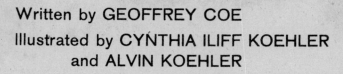

FISH

Written by GEOFFREY COE

Illustrated by CYNTHIA ILIFF KOEHLER
and ALVIN KOEHLER

Editorial Production: DONALD D. WOLF

Edited under the supervision of
Dr. Paul E. Blackwood,
Washington, D. C.

Text and illustrations approved by
Oakes A. White, Brooklyn Children's Museum,
Brooklyn, N. Y.

PRICE/STERN/SLOAN
Publishers, Inc., Los Angeles
1985

HATCHET FISH

Introduction

Most scientists believe that the origin of life was in the sea. The primeval forms of plant and animal life developed through countless ages in this watery home. Some forms became adapted to life on land and others remained bound to life in the sea. This *How and Why Wonder® Book of Fish* tells the story of the gradual development of life in the sea and the changes that led to eventual development of the fish families.

Fish have the same life functions as other animals. Though they move, eat, breathe and reproduce in ways that are peculiar to fish, countless variations among different kinds of fish enable them to live successfully in the sea. Some fish, for example, generate electric shocks to protect themselves. Others carry built-in head lights to penetrate the dark waters far below the surface. The eel and the salmon have elaborate migration patterns related to their life cycles. Indeed, the fantastic variations in structures and habits of fish must almost be seen to be believed.

This *How and Why Wonder® Book of Fish* will help young readers understand, as well as believe, the basic facts about various classes of fish and their fascinating patterns of life in the sea. It is a useful reference book for home and school use when boys and girls study this very important group of animals.

Paul E. Blackwood

Dr. Blackwood is a professional employee in the U. S. Office of Education. This book was edited by him in his private capacity and no official support or endorsement by the Office of Education is intended or should be inferred.

Contents

The Seas Are Formed

How did the earth get its water?

Many scientists believe that all early forms of life on earth began in the primeval seas. But before discussing the life of the seas, let us look at how the seas themselves came to be.

According to one scientific theory, the earth solidified out of clouds of cosmic dust into spheres of molten rock. Gases bubbled out of the hot interior and escaped into the cooler atmosphere that surrounded the earth. There they collected into vast clouds of water vapor. These clouds condensed and began to fall back upon the infant earth in the form of rain.

The earth's surface, however, was red-hot. As the raindrops touched it, they sizzled away — like drops of water spilled upon a hot stove — and returned to the upper atmosphere in the form of steam.

For millions of years the earth was

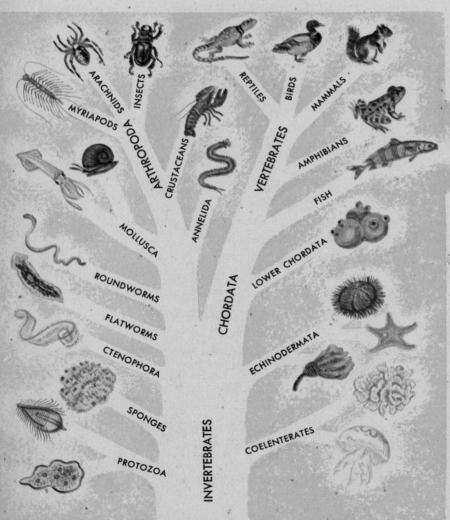

ANCESTRAL PROTOZOA

The illustration on the left gives you a simplified picture of the animal kingdom. The base of the tree represents the tiny, one-celled primitive forms of life, the ANCESTRAL PROTOZOA, from which all of the animals and plants of today have developed.

The simplest forms of animal life are at the bottom of the tree and the most developed forms are on the top. The big branches represent the main groups, or PHYLA; each phylum is divided into large groups or CLASSES, each class into ORDERS, each order into FAMILIES, each family into SPECIES. Our chart shows you only the phylum (the main branches of the tree), the class (the side-branches) and one typical representative of each class.

This should give you a general idea where the Fish stand within the animal kingdom. A line leads to the illustration on the right hand page. This gives you a detailed family tree of today's fish. The class, "Bony Fish" is broken down into FAMILIES.

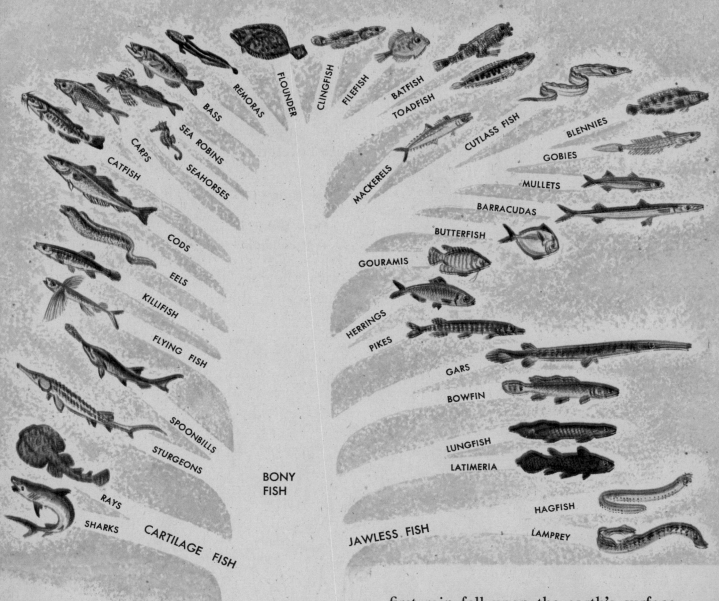

BASS
REMORAS
FLOUNDER
CLINGFISH
FILEFISH
BATFISH
TOADFISH
SEA ROBINS
SEAHORSES
CARPS
CATFISH
MACKERELS
CUTLASS FISH
BLENNIES
GOBIES
MULLETS
BARRACUDAS
BUTTERFISH
CODS
GOURAMIS
EELS
KILLIFISH
HERRINGS
PIKES
FLYING FISH
GARS
BOWFIN
SPOONBILLS
STURGEONS
LUNGFISH
LATIMERIA
BONY
FISH
RAYS
HAGFISH
SHARKS
CARTILAGE FISH
JAWLESS FISH
LAMPREY

Family tree of today's fish.

surrounded by a blanket of clouds many miles thick. These clouds were constantly condensing, falling to the earth as rain, and returning to the upper air as steam.

As these millions of years went by, the surface of the earth began to cool. Finally one day, many eons ago, the first rain fell upon the earth's surface without boiling away.

Then came a deluge. All of the water that had been collecting in the clouds for so long a time, fell upon the earth in an endless torrent. For thousands of years the stored-up rain poured down in a relentless cloudburst. There was no let-up, no minute of day or night when the merciless rain stopped. Lightning flashed through the sky, although there was no one to see it. The thunder roared, although there was no one to hear it.

5

The ceaseless downpour washed away some mountains and slashed out huge valleys in the newborn earth. The rains finally slowed and stopped. At last the sun shown down through a thin layer of clouds much as it does today. By this time, all the lowest parts of the earth's surface had been filled with the rainwater. The first seas were made.

What was the result of the deluge?

As the rains had washed over the earth's surface, they carried millions of tons of minerals away. These included iron, gold, silver, calcium, and vast quantities of salt. Mixed with the water, these minerals formed a sort of chemical "soup" in which the first forms of life developed.

How did life first develop?

This is a question that has not been definitely answered. One of the scientists' speculative theories suggests that certain of these chemical mixtures in the sea, exposed

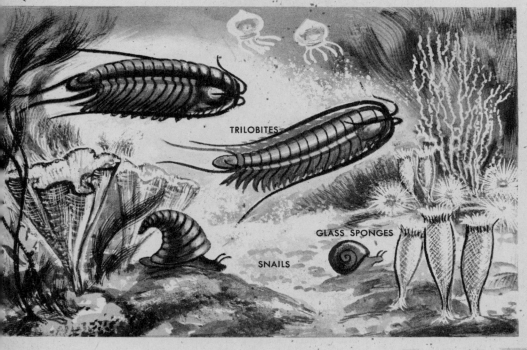

TRILOBITES

GLASS SPONGES

SNAILS

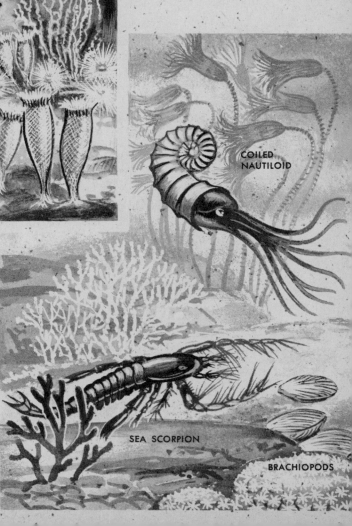

COILED NAUTILOID

SEA SCORPION

BRACHIOPODS

Only very few and sporadic traces of life can be found for periods earlier than the Cambrian period (about 500 million years ago). At that time, sea life was already considerably advanced. The most characteristic representatives of the Cambrian Seas were the trilobites that were living with the primitive snails and glass sponges.

100 million years after the Cambrian period, during the Silurian period, the forms of life had again advanced considerably. Many more creatures, more complex in organization and more varied in forms, inhabited the seas. Both illustrations are artists' conceptions of how the waters might have looked at these times.

to the heat of the sun, were somehow formed into a sort of bacteria that were capable of reproducing themselves. It is possible that these bacteria eventually developed into blue-green algae.

Developing from this algae, or perhaps developing independently at the same time, was a curious half-plant, half-animal creature called a protozoa. These creatures evolved into millions of shapes and forms. In general they must have looked like microscopic jellyfish.

Protozoa still make up the great bulk of life in the sea. They are so small that they can be seen only through a microscope. A single drop of sea water contains thousands of them, a glassful millions and millions.

Just how these tiny protozoa developed into the fish that we know today is another mystery that scientists have yet to solve. Perhaps this problem may never be solved.

All we know definitely is that several millions of years later, the seas became crowded with a vast number of life forms that were the primeval ancestors of many of the sea creatures with which we are familiar today.

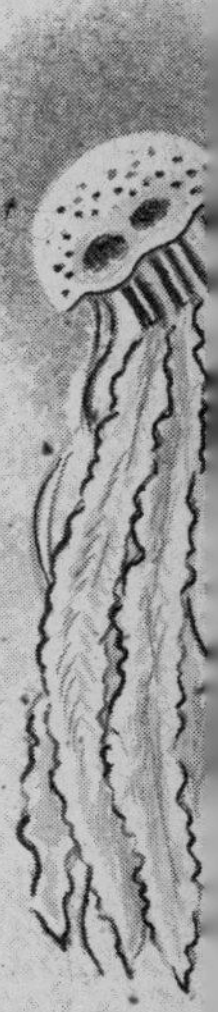

EARLY JELLYFISH

Sea Life Takes Form

Pictured here are a few of the first primitive "creatures." These creatures are the first forms of sea life of which we have any records. They lived in what scientists call the *Cambrian* Period, about 500 million years ago.

What was the Cambrian Period?

During this period, there were no true fish in the sea. Most animal life took the form of jellyfish, worms, snails, and crab-like creatures that had shells on the outside of their bodies.

All life in the sea was small at this time. There was still no life on the land. The trilobite, most populous of all the sea's animals, was only three inches long. The giant trilobite, perhaps the largest animal alive at that time, measured no more than eighteen inches.

As millions of years slowly continued to pass, the forms of the living things in the sea gradually changed. By the time of the *Silurian* period, some 350

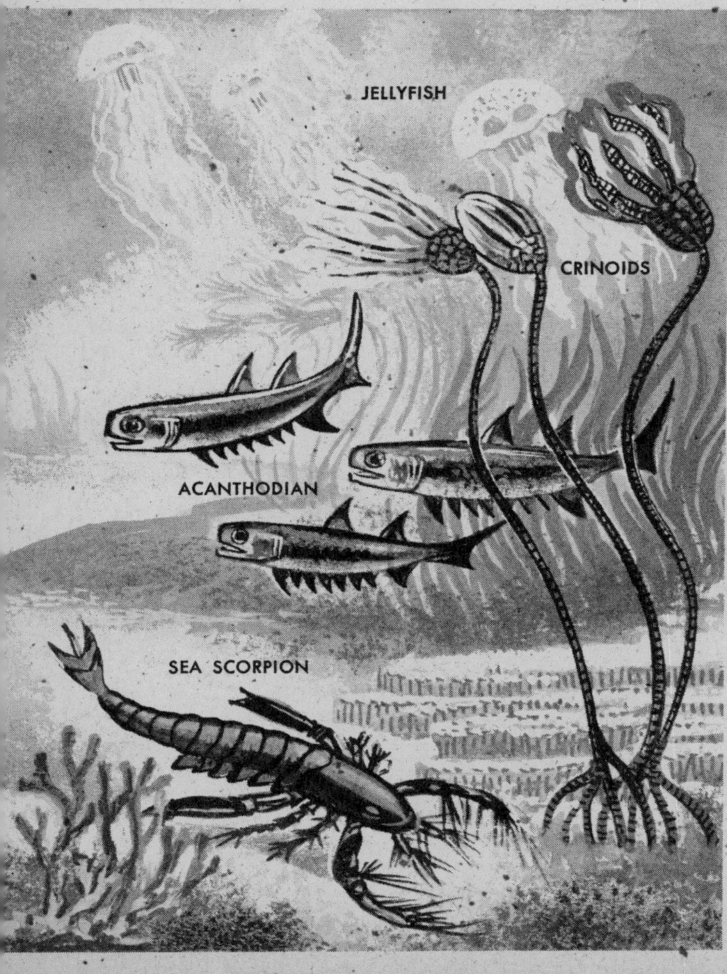

JELLYFISH

CRINOIDS

ACANTHODIAN

SEA SCORPION

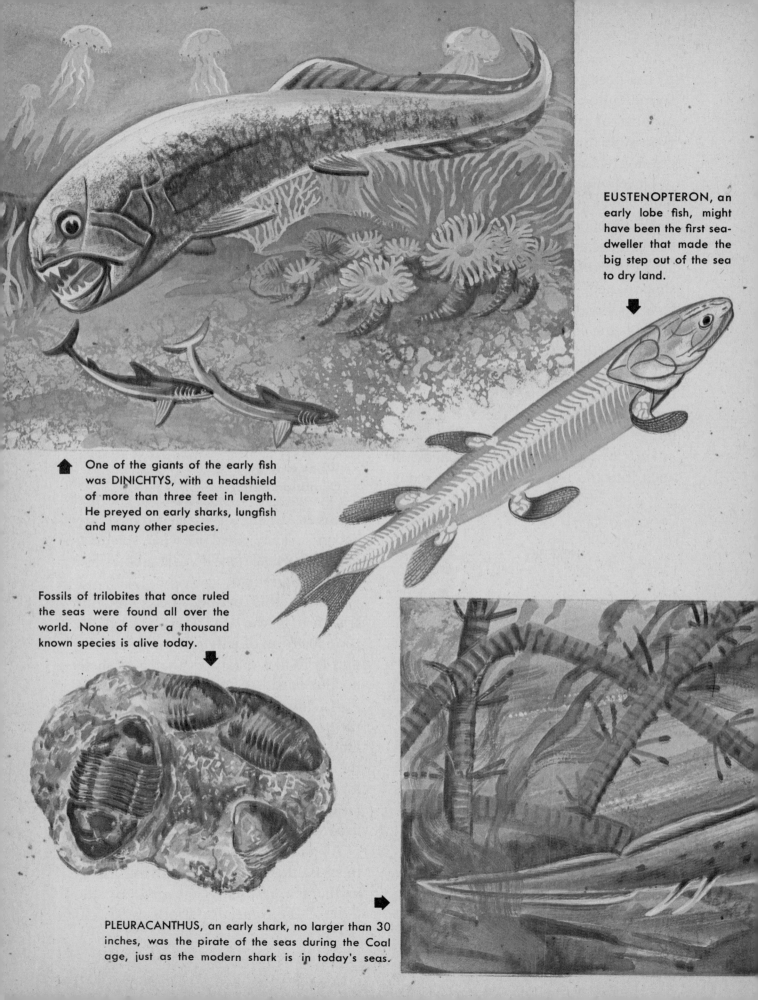

EUSTENOPTERON, an early lobe fish, might have been the first sea-dweller that made the big step out of the sea to dry land.

One of the giants of the early fish was DINICHTYS, with a headshield of more than three feet in length. He preyed on early sharks, lungfish and many other species.

Fossils of trilobites that once ruled the seas were found all over the world. None of over a thousand known species is alive today.

PLEURACANTHUS, an early shark, no larger than 30 inches, was the pirate of the seas during the Coal age, just as the modern shark is in today's seas.

million years ago, the trilobites, once the lords of the deep, had begun to disappear. The new royalty of the sea floor were the sea scorpions. Most of these were only an inch or two in length, but some giant species were as long as nine feet.

During the Silurian period, the protozoa and the jellyfish drifted on the sea's surface. The worms and various shellfish such as clams and trilobites either crawled or lay motionless on the bottom. They were unable to swim and it was not necessary for them to do so.

But in the waters of the inland lakes

What evolved in the Silurian Period?

and rivers, a new type of water animal was evolving. Scientists believe that these species developed from freshwater spineless creatures. They became streamlined, developed flexible fins,

125 million years after the Silurian age, during the Permian age of the world, fish-like reptiles shared the seas with the fish. Sea-reptiles like the ferocious Sea Lizard shown above, already had made the return trip from land-living to sea-dwelling. They looked like today's crocodiles, but were only about 30 inches long. In spite of the superficial likeness to crocodiles, they are not their ancestors.

sharp teeth and movable jaws. These were the first true fish.

In time, some of them migrated down the rivers to the oceans and gradually took over the vast middle areas of the seas, between the bottom and the surface, which until then had been uninhabited. The first of these true fish, the *acanthodian*, appeared in the seas late in the Silurian period.

Over millions of years, the acanthodian developed into two classes. One class became the ancestors of the sharks, skates, and rays that have skeletons of cartilage rather than bone. The other class evolved into the true, or boney, fish. These include tuna, mackeral, bass, trout, and all the other fish we eat as food today. There are now over 20,000 species of true fish, and they are the common denizens of the deep.

A few fish of the Silurian period have not changed very much to this day. The worms, snails and clams have not altered drastically in appearance. The horseshoe crab looks a great deal like his ancient ancestor, the trilobite, and the modern squid resembles the ancient coiled nautiloid.

The "Picture Book" of Fossils

How do we know what these ancient creatures were like? As the creatures of the primeval seas died, their bodies sank into the mud and silt of the ocean floor. Here the sea currents covered them with still more mud and silt. As millions of years passed, the pressure of the water and of the upper layers of silt slowly hardened this sediment into rock. The bodies of the dead creatures decayed and disappeared, but the outline of their forms was preserved forever in the rock.

Then pressures from inside the earth slowly bent the rock and in places lifted it out of the water. What was once sea bottom often became dry land. By looking at these uplifted rocks we are able to see the fossils of the ancient sea animals in what scientists call the "picture book" of rocks.

These layers of fossil-bearing rock have been piled one upon another for millions of years. Usually the oldest layers are on the bottom and the newer ones on top. By observing the sequence of rock layers, scientists can place the fossils in their proper time period.

The Grand Canyon of the Colorado River in Arizona is one of scientists' favorite places for studying these fossil remains. The plateau through which the canyon runs did not lift itself out of the sea in a violent upheaval as did so many other parts of the land that once were ocean floor. Instead it rose up so gradually that the rock layers were hardly tilted or twisted at all.

For this reason, the layers of fossil-bearing rock present a clear and accurate history of sea life, going back hundreds of millions of years. If you ride on a mule along the narrow, twisting trails that wind from the rim to the canyon floor, you pass through a living "picture book" of the development of life in the sea.

Some Fish Turn into Land Animals

The Silurian Period was followed by the

When did fish leave the sea?

Devonian Period about 300 million years ago. It was during this era that the first plants began to creep out of the seas and grow in the swamps and marshes along the shore. As the ages passed, they gradually changed from simple seaweeds into ferns and trees.

It was about the same time too, that certain species of fish learned to breathe air instead of extracting their oxygen from water. Gradually, their fins grew strong, like legs, and they could drag themselves out of the sea and start to live in the mud of the bogs and swamps. In the course of time, they developed into amphibians and reptiles. As more millions of years passed, these small reptiles evolved into the giant dinosaurs that roamed the earth so long ago.

Then for some curious reason, a number of these air-breathing land animals returned to the sea, which had originally been their home. Just as their fins had gradually strengthened into legs, now the process was reversed and the legs once more became fins. However, because they continued to breathe air, they did not go all the way back to being true fish again. Whales, porpoises, and sea turtles are the descendents of land creatures that made the return trip to their ancestral home in the sea.

The Fish of Today's Seas

By scientific definition, a *fish* is a cold-

What is a fish?

blooded water-dwelling animal, with a backbone and a skeleton. It breathes oxygen from the water through gills and has a mouth armed with teeth. A fish moves by swimming.

Fish are further grouped into two subclasses:

The *elasmobranchii* have skeletons of cartilage instead of bone. These are the sharks, rays and mantas.

The *teleostomi* have skeletons of bone, and are buoyed up in the water by means of air bladders inside their bodies. They are the common fish such as trout, bass, cod, herring, eel and the like. They are known as true fish.

It is generally accepted, however, that almost all water-dwelling creatures are referred to as "fish." The lamprey and hagfish are known as primitive fish. Clams, oysters, and crabs are called shellfish. The starfish, for exam-

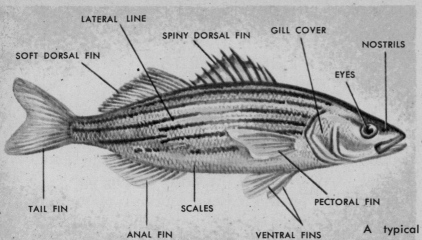

LATERAL LINE

SOFT DORSAL FIN

SPINY DORSAL FIN

GILL COVER

NOSTRILS

EYES

TAIL FIN

SCALES

PECTORAL FIN

ANAL FIN

VENTRAL FINS

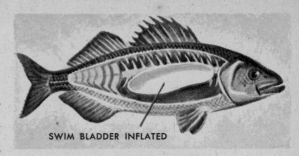

SWIM BLADDER INFLATED

The illustration shows the location of the swim bladder with the organ inflated; the illustration on the opposite page shows the swim bladder deflated.

A typical bony fish with the identification of its parts.

ple, is not a fish at all; but because he is shaped like a star and lives on the bottom of the sea, he got this name.

Fish of various kinds are found in all the fresh and salt waters of the world except in places where the water is poisonous or contaminated. For instance, in the Dead Sea, in Palestine, the water is so salty that no life at all can exist. In Utah's Great Salt Lake, there are only a few primitive worms. In some streams near industrial areas, the water has been so contaminated by chemical wastes that fish life has been wiped out entirely. But for the most part, wherever you find a body of water, you will also find fish.

Fish species in the sea exceed the num-

Why are they so much alike?

ber of animal species on the land (excluding insects). The fish are also more primitive and less diversified than their land relatives. This is largely due to the fact that the sea, changing little from place to place or century to century, provides a more consistent environment than the land. The fish have not been forced to

adapt themselves, as have the land animals, to such severe contrasts of living conditions as desert and swamp, or arctic sub-freezing cold and tropical heat. Although in places the sea is more than six miles deep, most species live in shallow waters or in the upper strata of deep waters. Here the temperatures vary only a few degrees from the arctic to the equator.

The vast waters of the sea are teeming with food. The tiniest fish feed on the protozoa and seaweed; then the bigger fish eat the smaller ones. And so it goes on up the scale, with each smaller fish serving as food for one stronger than itself. Fish rarely starve because they have no trouble finding abundant food.

The sea, however, does have certain boundaries that form specific habitats for certain types of fish. These boundaries are the saltiness in the water, slight changes in temperature, and the water pressure itself. Unlike many land animals, most fish cannot adapt themselves to a changing environment. A sudden shift in an ocean current, bringing warm water into an area where the

A cutaway view of a bony fish, identifying the parts and location of the organs.

By increasing or decreasing the amount of air in the bladder, the fish changes the weight of air in the bladder, enabling him to rise or sink.

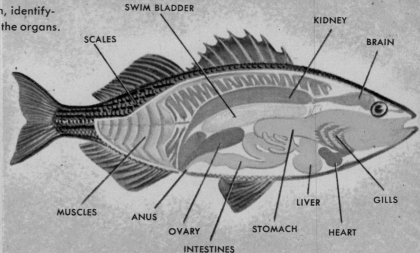

SWIM BLADDER DEFLATED

How do fish swim?

water had been slightly colder, may wipe out huge segments of the under water population.

The body of a true, or boney, fish is heavier than the volume of the water that it displaces. Under normal circumstances, therefore, it would tend to sink. But the true fish has an air bladder inside its body that gives it buoyancy and makes it float in the water.

This air bladder is connected by a delicate mechanism to the fish's inner ear, just as the inner ear of a human being enables him to keep his balance. When the fish swims into deep water, the pressure on its inner ear is increased. This action automatically increases the volume of air in the bladder and enables it to maintain its equilibrium at any normal depth.

A shark is also heavier than the water that it displaces but it has no air bladder to buoy it up. Therefore, it must constantly be swimming in order to keep from sinking.

A fish gains forward motion by creating water currents around it with its

JELLYFISH   STARFISH

CRAYFISH   CUTTLEFISH

Above are four "fish" that are not fish.

tail, and steers itself up and down and from side to side with its fins in the same way that a bird glides to and fro through the air by changing the position of its wings in flight.

Many fish can swim very swiftly. Certain types of salmon have been clocked by observers, and have been found to be able to swim as fast as a good athlete can run — that is, about one hundred

Head of the fish with gill cover removed. Most bony fish have four pair of gills. The blood is very close to the surface of the thin skin of the gills, enabling the oxygen to go from the water into the blood.

WATER IN

WATER OUT

GILL COVER (PARTLY CUT AWAY)

GILLS

Land animals get their oxygen from the air; fish take the oxygen from the water with their gills. The water enters the fish's mouth, is carried around the gills and leaves the body through slits behind the gill covers.

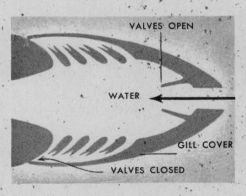

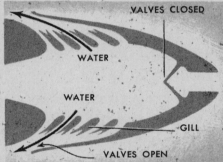

VALVES OPEN

WATER

GILL COVER

VALVES CLOSED

VALVES CLOSED

WATER

WATER

GILL

VALVES OPEN

There are valves on the gill covers which regulate the flow of water around the gills. When the gill covers move outward, water is drawn into the mouth; when the gill covers move inward, the water is forced out.

yards in ten seconds. However, they cannot maintain this speed for very long.

How do fish breathe?

All animals must breathe oxygen into their blood streams in order to live. Both air and water contain large quantities of oxygen. A land animal takes in this oxygen from the air by means of its lungs. A fish extracts oxygen from the water by means of its gills.

The lungs of a man cannot separate oxygen from water. Therefore, if a man is kept under water for more than a few minutes, he dies. Similarly, a fish's gills cannot extract oxygen from air. And so

the fish quickly dies if it is kept out of the water.

A fish takes in water through its mouth. As the water passes out through the gills in the sides of its head, the oxygen from the water is retained and passes into the fish's bloodstream. (The lungs of a man retain oxygen from the air, and pump it into his bloodstream.) If you look at a fish in a glass tank, you can see that the intake valves in its mouth and its gill openings are constantly working. This is because the fish is breathing, just as you are constantly inhaling and exhaling air.

In the fish world, like almost everywhere else, there are exceptions which prove the rule. In Africa, South America and Australia, there are fish called lungfish that are able to breathe both underwater and in the open air. In fact, some of them can bury themselves in the mud of swamps and river banks and live for months at a time. These strange fish are the last living link between the animals of the land and those of the sea.

Why are fish called cold-blooded?

The temperature of a mammal, including man, remains fairly constant at all times. Your normal temperature, for example, is approximately 98.6 degrees. As long as you are healthy, this temperature never changes. If you go out in extremely cold weather, you wear warm clothing to protect yourself from the colder outdoor temperature.

In the same way, a polar bear grows a thick layer of fat all over its body to keep its blood warm when swimming in icy Arctic seas.

The temperature of a fish's blood, however, fluctuates with the temperature of the surrounding water. It has no constant degree of heat. A bass can live comfortably in the warm water of a lake in summer, or under the ice when the lake freezes over in winter.

Snakes and frogs have this same characteristic. Along with fish, they are known as "cold-blooded" animals.

Does a fish ever sleep?

Because fish have no eyelids, they are never able to close their eyes. But nonetheless, they frequently rest in a sort of trance which we would call sleep. They never "sleep" very soundly, as humans often do, for the slightest disturbance in the water will arouse them. If you happen to see a fish lying motionless in the water, it is very likely that it is "asleep."

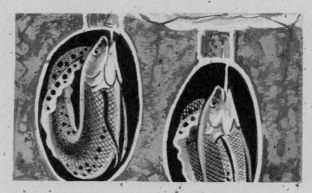

AFRICAN LUNGFISH

Mudskippers can take oxygen directly out of the air. They move on land by using their fins and tails to crawl.

15

We know that fish can certainly see, and

Does a fish see, hear and smell? many people believe that fish can tell one color from another. A trout will gobble up a brightly colored fly that is dangled in the water before him, yet ignore one that is of a different color.

But in spite of the fact that the eyes of most fish are extremely large, they probably cannot see very well. The pupils of their eyes are large in order to admit as much as possible of the light that filters down through the water.

Fish have no outer ears, but they are able to detect sound waves that are sent through the water.

We also know that fish such as sharks and barracuda are attracted to the smell of blood in water, sometimes from as great a distance as half a mile or more.

Most fish live in a world of silence, but

Do fish make sounds? several of them do make sounds as they swim through the water. Mostly these sounds are the result of one part of the fish's skeleton rubbing against another, or of air being expelled from the swim bladder.

The *drum,* a large fish, gets its name because it makes a drumming sound that can be heard from a distance of several yards. *Sea robins, singing midshipmen,* and *toadfish* make a squeaking sound like a frightened mouse. Some fish make noises when they are disturbed, and it is thought that the *river catfish* may communicate with others of its kind by making noises in the thick, muddy water where it cannot see.

The biggest of all fish is the *whale shark*

How big do fish grow? (see page 20), which grows to a length of fifty feet or more, and weighs several tons.

The biggest freshwater fish is the *pirarucu,* also called arapaima, of South America. It often weighs more than 400 pounds.

The world's smallest fish is a type of *goby* found in the lakes and rivers of the Philippine Islands. When fully grown, it is less than one-half inch in length. It is generally considered to be the smallest vertebrate in the world.

When a lake or pond freezes, only

How can fish live in a frozen pond? the surface is covered with ice. The fish live in the water underneath the ice. As we have seen, fish regulate the temperature of their bodies to that of the surrounding water; they experience no discomfort from the cold.

But they have another problem. The cover of ice may keep oxygen from passing out of the air into the water. Unless a supply of fresh water keeps coming into the pond from under the ice, the oxygen may soon be used up.

It is for this same reason that pet goldfish or other tropical fish can die in a tank of water. The surface of the water may not absorb enough oxygen from the air to keep the fish alive. Then, as a fish uses up the supply of oxygen in the water, it literally "drowns." That is why, if you keep pet fish, you must frequently change the water in order to give them a fresh oxygen supply.

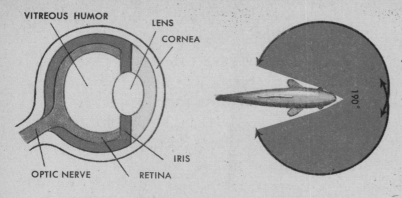

VITREOUS HUMOR
LENS
CORNEA
OPTIC NERVE
RETINA
IRIS

190°

A fish's eye (left) and its wide field of vision (right).

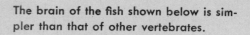

The brain of the fish shown below is simpler than that of other vertebrates.

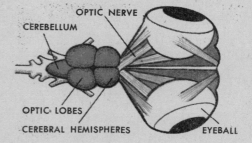

OPTIC NERVE
CEREBELLUM
OPTIC LOBES
CEREBRAL HEMISPHERES
EYEBALL

The STICKLEBACK builds a nest.

The TOADFISH (at right) lays its eggs in a protected spot and watches over them until they hatch.

Development of the Fish

The majority of fish species lay their eggs in the water. The females of some species, however, carry the eggs until they have hatched, and then give birth to the young. (Some even carry the young after they have left the egg.) Some fish lay their eggs in the open water and don't care for the young; others build a kind of nest and guard the eggs until they hatch. With a few species either the mother or the father stays with the young until they are able to take care of themselves.

Below, as an example of the growth of a typical bony fish, the development of the COD from an egg, that hatches in 20-40 days, to the young fish approximately six months old.

EGG

NEWLY HATCHED

LARVA AFTER A FEW WEEKS

YOUNG COD

SCALES

The body of the mature fish is covered with scales. The scales in turn are, in most fish, covered with a thin layer of skin. Many little glands within this skin secrete a slime that covers the fish and protects it against fungi and other parasites.

CYCLOID SCALES

CTENOID SCALES

PLACOID SCALES

GANOID SCALES

The scales increase in size with the age of the fish. The form and size of scales vary in different species. Scientists group scales into 4 main groups: placoid scales (toothlike, as with sharks), ganoid scales (platelike, as with primitive fish), cycloid (smooth) and ctenoid (rough with comb-like edges).

17

Some fish, such as halibut, herring, and swordfish, live in salt water. Others, such as pickerel, perch, and lake trout, live in fresh water. If a saltwater fish is placed in fresh water, it will quickly die. If a freshwater fish is placed in salt water, it, too, may die, although some freshwater fish can adapt to a more salty environment.

How do freshwater and saltwater fish differ?

Some kinds of fish spend part of the time in fresh water and part in salt water. Eels live in fresh water for most of their life, then swim out to sea to spawn. Salmon, some trout, shad, sturgeon and other fish mature in the salty ocean, then return to freshwater rivers to spawn. Some fish, such as smelt and stickleback, inhabit the half-salty waters where rivers meet the ocean.

Whether a fish lives in fresh or salt water depends on its internal organs. A fish must maintain a certain concentration of salt in its body fluids — less than the salt in ocean water, more than the salt in fresh water. Fish are constantly absorbing some of the water they swim in. The skin of a fish is porous; water can seep through it. Water also passes through a fish's gills, and water enters its stomach, along with food. Freshwater fish absorb more fresh water than their body needs. To keep this fresh water from washing away the salt in their body, they eliminate the absorbed water through their kidneys as quickly as possible. Whatever salt is needed is extracted from the water through their gills.

A saltwater fish must obtain fresh water from its salty surroundings, and must keep this water within its body. Cartilaginous fishes, such as sharks, retain *urea,* a waste product that prevents the loss of their body fluids. Bony saltwater fish also tend to lose body water through their skin and gills. To counterbalance this, they drink large quantities of sea water. They remove the salt by excreting it through special cells in their gills, and retain as much of the desalinated water as possible.

When salmon leave the ocean and swim upriver to spawn, their digestive organs no longer function and they need little water. This allows them to survive in the fresh river waters long enough to spawn before they die. Similarly, when eels enter the ocean, their skin becomes coated with mucus that prevents the loss of body water. In these various ways fish maintain the salt-and-water balance they require.

The Jawless Fish

Jawless fish are very primitive. They have no jaws, no bones, no paired fins, no nervous system, and no scales. There are only two kinds of these jawless fish — *hagfish* and *lampreys*. Both are scavengers and parasites.

How do they eat?

MOUTH OF A LAMPREY

The *hagfish* attaches itself to the body of a large foodfish, such as a haddock, cod, or mackeral, and drills into it with

LAMPREY

its sharp, rasplike teeth. Working like a termite, it eats away the insides of the victim, leaving the exterior intact. When the fish is dead, the hag attaches itself to another unlucky live meal.

Hags are found in both the Atlantic and Pacific Oceans, and are a real menace to commercial fishermen. The hag is blind, and locates its prey by an unusually keen sense of smell. A wormlike, saltwater fish, usually from one to two feet long, it is found at depths ranging from 100 to about 3,000 feet. Often the hag burrows into the mud and waits for its prey to swim by.

The *lamprey* is an eel-like fish that grows up to three feet long. It eats by attaching itself to the body of a larger fish with its suction mouth and sucking out the blood and other life juices.

Lampreys are normally saltwater fish, but they move up the freshwater streams and into inland lakes to spawn. They can even ascend waterfalls by attaching their mouths to rocks and pulling themselves upward. At the spawning place, the male and female build a nest of rocks, and in it the female lays some

200,000 eggs. After the male has fertilized them, both parents die.

Sometimes lampreys stay permanently in the inland lakes and never go back to sea. When this happens, they can do serious damage.

About thirty years ago, commercial fishing was a prosperous industry in the Great Lakes area, with a yearly catch of about eleven million pounds of lake trout and other freshwater fish. Then the lampreys moved into the Great Lakes and virtually destroyed all the fish. Today there is a minimum of commercial fishing in these waters. The United States Bureau of Fisheries is now conducting a widespread program aimed at controlling these pests.

Lampreys look like eels and are often called "lamprey eels." But, being jawless fish, they are in no way related to the eel family. In the Middle Ages, European lampreys were esteemed as great delicacies. However, they are no longer caught for food.

The Cartilage Fish — Sharks and Rays

Sharks are the killer wolves of the sea.

Do they have bones? Many species will attack anything that moves in the water, from human swimmers to whales. They have been known to attack boats which they mistook for large fish. Often, they savagely fight with and kill each other. One of the most ferocious of the species is the *great white shark,* commonly called the maneater.

Sharks are not true fish, since their skeletons are made of cartilage instead of bone; also, their gill slits are behind their heads, slightly above the pectoral fins, instead of in the sides of their heads.

The *mako,* another maneater, is first cousin to the great white shark. It has rows of long frightening teeth set in powerful jaws that, with one bite, are capable of snapping a man or a big fish in two. Often, the mako prefers to swallow his food in a single gulp. On one occasion, a 120 pound swordfish was found whole in the stomach of a 730 pound mako.

The *whale shark,* biggest of all the sharks, grows to lengths of fifty feet or more and may weigh several tons. In

WHALE SHARK

THRESHER SHARK

SAWFISH

WHITE SHARK

HAMMERHEAD

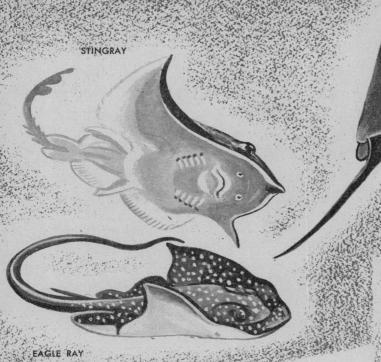

STINGRAY

GREAT MANTA

EAGLE RAY

MAKO SHARK, a maneater like the White Shark.

spite of its tremendous size, the whale shark lives on a diet of tiny fish like shrimps and other small crustaceans. It swallows whole schools of little fish at once. The fish are then filtered out by a series of strainers, and are digested and the water continues out through the gills of the shark.

Although it does not use them for eating, the whale shark has thousands of very small teeth in its huge frog-like head. Whale sharks are lazy and slow. Many cases have been reported of sailing ships ramming into them when the great creatures were calmly swimming and feeding just under the surface.

The curious *basking shark* is almost as big as the whale shark. This giant among fish is often seen swimming lazily along the surface of the ocean with its dorsal fin protruding out of the water. Sometimes it lies on its side, bask-

ing in the sun, or turns over on its back. When it is taking a sun bath in this manner, its white belly can be seen from very far away.

The basking shark, in spite of its size, does not eat other fish at all. Instead, it lives entirely on a diet of plankton, the microscopic plant and animal life of the sea. Like the whale shark, it has a series of strainers that filter out the food as the water passes through its gills.

The liver of a basking shark com-

prises one-tenth of its entire weight, and is rich in oil. As much as six hundred gallons of oil have been extracted from the liver of a single basking shark. This oil does not contain vitamins, as does the liver of the cod. It is used chiefly for tanning leather.

The *thresher shark* has a scythe-shaped tail, which is usually about as long as its body. It obtains its food by flailing its great tail on the surface of the water. The splashing drives schools of little fish into a close huddle. The thresher circles round and round, herding the fish into a compact mass. At last it dashes into the midst of the school, and eats up its victims by the hundreds. The thresher is a menace to other fish, but harmless to human swimmers.

The *hammerhead* is the oddest looking of all the shark family. Its eyes are set on each side of its hammer-shaped head which it swings from side to side as it rapidly swims about, looking for prey. The hammerhead is extremely dangerous to humans.

The *sawfish* carries a long, bone-like saw on the end of its snout, which it uses to club its victims to death. The saw of an adult is about three feet long, and is armed with sharp teeth. This shark swims rapidly through a school of smaller fish, lashing out with its fearful weapon. After it has killed several dozen victims in this manner, the sawfish cruises about eating the dead prey at leisure.

The *stingray* has often been called the "rattlesnake" of the sea. It carries a poisonous sting on the end of its long tail which can cause death to a human in a matter of hours. This ray, which is shaped like a small boy's long-tailed kite, lives on a diet of crabs, clams, lobsters and other animals of the sea bottom, which it crushes with its powerful grinder teeth.

The *great manta* is the largest of all the ray-type sharks. A full-sized adult weighs nearly two tons. Although they are sometimes called "devilfish," they are not dangerous to humans. Many skin divers have climbed up on their broad backs and been taken on long rides through the water. If the manta is frightened, however, it can smash a small boat with one flap of its wing-like fins. This giant of the shark family eats only crabs, lobsters and small fish.

"Mermaid's purse" is the egg case of a shark embryo. The round yolk in the purse provides nourishment for the shark until it hatches.

There are 250 species of shark in the oceans, but only about two dozen of these are dangerous to man. The man-eaters are usually found in tropical waters, and are especially numerous in the Caribbean, the Indian Ocean, and the waters around Australia and South Africa. They are rarely seen in places where the water temperature is lower than 65° F. Occasionally some sharks may follow a warm current northward, away from the tropics. Although sharks are saltwater fish (except for one species), sharks sometimes wander upriver for great distances.

Are sharks dangerous?

Sharks are "living garbage cans." Because of their poor vision and low intelligence, they will often attack and swallow shiny pieces of metal, bright clothing, cartons, as well as birds, turtles, and humans. The shark is well-equipped to eat almost anything. Its mouth has double rows of razor-sharp teeth that can chew up even a large animal in a very short time. When the front teeth are broken or worn down, the rear teeth move forward to replace them.

Experiments have shown that sharks have an excellent sense of smell which enables them to detect blood or other savory odors at a distance of several hundred feet. Using its nose, the shark homes in on its prey until it is a dozen feet away. Then its sense of sight takes over. From the moment a shark starts to wheel around for its attack, it rarely stops until it

How do sharks spot their prey?

has gobbled up its prey. Sometimes a wounded fish releases so much blood in the water that many other sharks are drawn to the area. Excited by the kill, the sharks may attack each other in a furious "feeding frenzy."

Much research has been done to develop a "shark chaser" — a chemical that a swimmer could use to repel sharks. Many chemicals were tried in the hope of confusing the sharks' sense of smell, but none was effective. A deep blue-black dye around a swimmer can provide some protection because it reduces the shark's vision, but the shark is not repelled. Underwater horn sounds also fail to drive away sharks. In fact, it has been found that erratic thumping noises, like the flutter of a dying fish, actually attract sharks. That's why killing one shark often draws many other sharks to the scene. Scientists have experimented with an underwater gun that shoots a tranquilizing dart into a shark, so that it sinks quietly to the bottom without attracting other sharks.

Can sharks be repelled?

For a long time it was thought that a curtain of air bubbles pumped through an underwater pipe could protect a beach or harbor against sharks, but these "bubble curtains" eventually proved ineffective. The only real protection for bathers is a net of wire cable placed around the swimming area, though sharks can sometimes slip around the net. But it should be realized that the danger of sharks to bathers is often exaggerated.

The Bony Fish

FOOD FISH

Why are food fish important to man? The fish of the sea provide mankind's greatest source of food. In many nations such as Japan, China, Iceland, Southern Italy, Greece and the Scandinavian countries, fish is virtually the only meat that is eaten. The most important food fish are *cod, herring, tuna, salmon,* and *flounder*. Some species, like the mackerel, travel together in schools so large that a single school may cover several square miles of ocean.

The *cod* is one of the most important of all the food fish. It is a fairly large fish, growing to be three or four feet long and weighing from five to twelve pounds.

ALBACORE TUNA

SPOTTED JEWFISH

ELECTRIC CATFISH

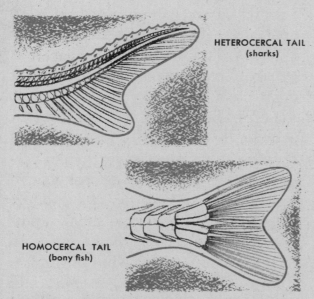

HETEROCERCAL TAIL
(sharks)

HOMOCERCAL TAIL
(bony fish)

The tails of the primitive fish of today compared with other species show the development that the skeleton has undergone. In the shark and in fossils, the backbone extends to the tip of the tail; in bony fish the backbone ends where the tail begins.

Various types of *tuna* are found all over the world, and the individual schools themselves migrate for great distances. The largest of the tunas, the *giant bluefin*, attains a length of fourteen feet and a weight of nearly one ton. Tuna packed in cans are usually albacore, yellowfin, or skipjack.

The *flounder* is an odd-looking fish that appears to have been run over and smashed flat by a steamroller. When it is first hatched from the egg, a baby flounder looks like any other newborn fish, and swims about normally.

Then, in a few days, a curious thing

BLUEFIN TUNA

TOM COD

BLACK SEA BASS

STRIPED BASS

POMPANO

MARINE CATFISH

STURGEON

HERRING

SARDINES

begins to happen. One eye starts moving to the opposite side of the head, and soon the little flounder has two eyes on the same side. Its body begins to flatten out, and the fish starts to swim on its side, with the two-eyed side up. The blind side loses its pigmentation and becomes a sort of colorless white, while the "seeing" side develops many colors. Some flounders have the ability to change their coloring to match the sea floor and thus protect themselves.

The *sea bass* is a common and delicious food fish. There are about 400 species in the bass family, and they range in size from about one ounce to more than a thousand pounds in weight.

The *striped bass* is found in the shallow waters of the sea close to shore, and swims up the coastal rivers to lay its eggs in the sand. This is a colorful and spirited fish, and is a favorite among sportsmen who angle with rod and reel from an open boat.

The *jewfish*, or giant sea bass, is the largest of this widespread fish family. The biggest ever netted weighed 800 pounds, and the largest ever caught with sporting tackle weighed 551 pounds.

The *sardine* is a member of the herring family. These little fish, which we eat whole from cans, provide not only an important item of food for humans, but also the chief source of food for some of the bigger fish in the sea.

The *herrings* move in tremendous schools, and the entire school swims together with military precision. Strangely enough, in the northern hemisphere, herring schools move in a clockwise direction. In waters south of the equator, they move counter-clockwise.

The *sturgeon* is a huge, very fierce-looking fish that resembles a shark in many ways. Many sturgeons have been caught that weighed more than two thousand pounds. But in spite of its ferocious appearance, the sturgeon is not fierce at all. Underneath its soft, toothless mouth are a set of long feelers used to find food. The sturgeon eats snails, crawfish and small fish which it sucks up into its mouth while cruising along the sea bottom.

The sturgeon is valued for its flesh, but its chief contribution to man's food supply is its eggs. These eggs are processed and sold under the name of caviar, one of the costliest and tastiest delicacies that we get from the sea.

The *catfish* is found, in many varied forms, all over the world, in both fresh and salt water. In the eastern United States, the catfish is a favorite catch for sport fishermen, and constitutes an important food item.

Catfish have long feelers extending from each side of the head, and sharp spines along their backs that can painfully stab a careless fisherman. One species, the *electric catfish*, is found in African rivers. It is a big fish, weighing as much as fifty pounds, and can deliver an electric shock equal to one hundred volts. The ancient Egyptians considered them to be sacred, and carved pictures of them on the walls of tombs. Even so, they sometimes used the electric catfish for food, as do many African tribes.

The *pompano* is one of the prettiest and to many people, the most delicious of all the deep-sea food fish. It is a small fish, only about two or three pounds in weight, but it is highly esteemed as a table delicacy. Pompanos are found off the southern Atlantic coast of the United States and in the Gulf of Mexico. They bring very high prices in the market.

The mouth of the sturgeon on the underside of the head, forms a tubular opening.

DWELLERS OF THE DEEP

Since earliest recorded history, men have told tales of huge **How do fish see in the dark?** sea monsters lurking in the deep waters. Most of these stories have been dismissed as legends and myths.

But in recent years, scientists have been inclined to take a more open-minded view of this subject.

By means of a submarine device, called the bathyscaphe, men have descended to the lowest part of the ocean floor, the Marianas Trench in the Pacific, almost seven miles down. The bathyscaphe operates much like an aerial balloon; but whereas a balloon uses gas, which is lighter than air, for buoyancy, the bathyscaphe uses gasoline, which is lighter than water.

No light at all penetrates the sea below about 2,000 feet. Yet in this utter blackness, many strange fish swim about and hunt their prey.

Here is the only part of the sea where food is not plentiful. As a result, most deep-sea fish are equipped with large, gaping mouths and long sharp teeth to simplify catching their food. One species, the *chiasmodon*, has a distensible stomach that makes it possible to

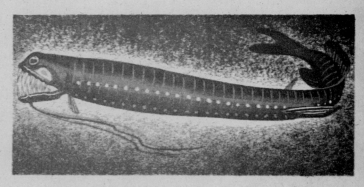

A monster of the ocean's abyss, the MELANOSTOMIAS MELANOPS trails lure from its lower jaw to attract its prey within the reach of its dangerous teeth.

Deep-sea angler fish carries a "lantern" on its upper jaw. The "cold light" of the lantern is created by luminescent chemicals like those in fireflies. The fish's lantern probably attracts its prey in the blackness of the deep ocean.

The lure at the end of a long rod above the mouth of GIGANTACTIS VANHOEFFENI is a device to attract the prey, which then is quickly seized.

CHIASMODON NIGER grows no longer than 2 inches, but is able to swallow fish bigger than itself, as indicated in the illustration.

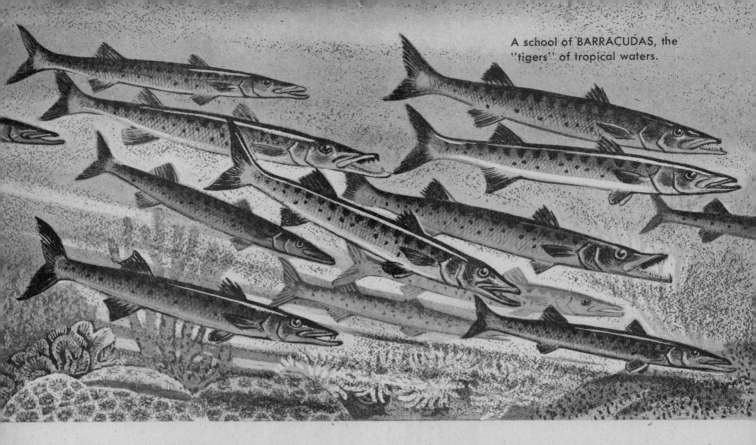

A school of BARRACUDAS, the "tigers" of tropical waters.

swallow other fish which are as much as three times larger than itself.

The *melanocetus,* or black angler, carries a bright light on the end of an antenna that sprouts from the middle of its forehead. This light attracts smaller fish into its huge mouth.

The *black whip-bearer* is covered with glowing spots and has a long whip-like antenna on the end of its nose. It uses this whip to find other fish in the darkness.

The *photostomias* has rows of bright lights along its long, slender body that glow like the lighted portholes of a ship.

The *gonostoma* trails a bright light on a long chin whisker.

These fish living in the great deep have adapted themselves to withstand the tremendous pressure. At a depth of 15,000 feet, the pressure of the water is about two and a half tons per square inch. A fish that normally lives near the surface would be squeezed into a pulp.

Can deep sea fish surface?

When a deep-sea fish swims upward, it sometimes rises too far. As it rises, the water pressure decreases and causes the gas in the fish's swimming bladder to expand, forcing the fish to keep on rising no matter how hard it tries not to. Near the surface, its internal organs may swell up so much that its body bursts.

But enough of these strange fish of the deep are caught in the nets of marine biologists and brought intact to the surface for us to know what a few of them look like.

RAINBOW TROUT

LAKE TROUT

BROOK TROUT

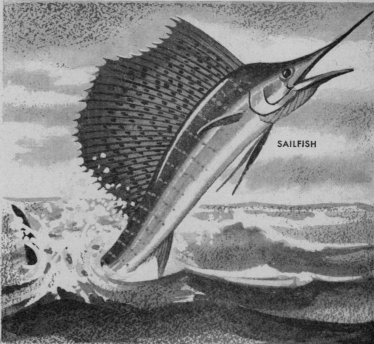

SAILFISH

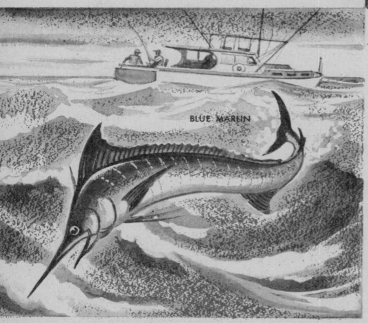

BLUE MARLIN

BONEFISH

LARGEMOUTH BASS

GAME FISH

There are certain fish that have always been especial favorites of man because it is so much fun to catch them with a rod and reel. Instead of submitting calmly to their fate

How did they get this name?

when hooked, these particular fish put up such a fight that very often they will get away from any but an expert angler. For this reason, we call them "game" fish. There is hardly an American boy or girl who has not spent a pleasant summer afternoon on the bank

29

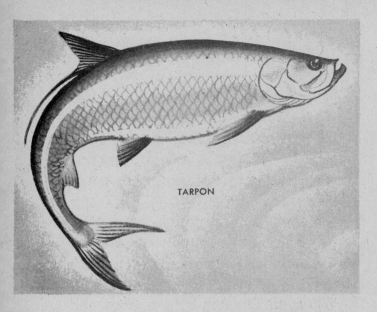
TARPON

of a pond or stream, successfully improving his skill as a fisherman.

Here are a few of these game fish, from both the sea and freshwater rivers and lakes, that are the most fun to catch.

The *bonefish* is a scrappy little fighter. Its average weight is only about five pounds, but sometimes it takes an expert fisherman as long as an hour to haul one in. Bonefish feed in shallow off-shore waters, sometimes barely deep enough to cover them completely. Here they search in the mud and sand for shrimps and small lobsters, their chief items of food. They are found in both the Atlantic and Pacific Oceans, but are most numerous around Florida and the Bahama Islands.

The *great barracuda* is often called the "tiger of the sea." It fears nothing that swims, and will attack anything, including man. Its jaws are lined with razor-sharp teeth that can take off a man's hand with one snap.

When a barracuda is hooked, it puts up a fight equalled by no other fish its size. Even after it is landed, it must be handled with care. Many a careless fisherman has lost a finger to a barracuda that has suddenly "come to life" after being put in the boat.

The *tarpon* is one of the most exciting fish to catch, although it has little value as food. When hooked, it rushes around in the water and leaps high into the air. Since some of these huge fish weigh 300 pounds or more, it takes great skill to land one. Tarpons are most commonly found in warm sub-tropical waters

The *blue marlin,* like the tarpon, is a furious fighter when hooked. Very large ones weigh up to 1,200 pounds. It is thrilling to see this big fish rushing at top speed through the water and leaping high into the air. Sometimes, when hooked, it will stand up on the surface almost to its full length. It keeps erect by lashing its great tail furiously. This is called "tail walking."

The *sailfish* is considered by many sportsmen to be the most beautiful of all of the ocean fish. It usually travels in small schools, with its large dorsal fin, or sail, folded down on its back. When it is hooked, it leaps high out of the water, and spreads its sail stiffly erect.

The *trout* is the favorite game fish among freshwater anglers. Most species are found in the cold water mountain streams. There are many kinds of trout, all beautifully colored. The loveliest is the *rainbow trout* which is decorated with all the hues and tints of the rainbow. Most trout stay in fresh water all their lives, except for one type, similar to the rainbow, called the *steelhead*. Like the salmon, it migrates downstream to the ocean and returns to fresh water to spawn.

Many fish swim together in orderly groups called "schools." The fish in a school move in unison and maintain the same speed, spacing, and direction. The reason for fish "schooling" behavior is not known.

Many types of fish swim together in groups called "schools." A school may have thousands of fish in it, or only a dozen. But a school is more than just a crowd of fish milling around. Anyone who has watched a school of minnows in the clear water beneath a pier has noticed that they all seem to face the same way, that they turn at the same time in the same direction, and that they swim at the same speed. A school of fish seems as well-organized as a column of marching soldiers. Yet, strangely enough, this well-disciplined group of fish has no leader; the fish are constantly changing places, although they are careful to stay the same distance from each other at all times.

Why do fish swim in schools?

Experiments have shown that fish learn to school very early in life. When they are newly hatched they tend to swim head-to-tail, but they soon learn parallel swimming. They quickly form into large groups that stay together and move in unison. Apparently, vision is the key to fish schooling. Each fish watches the fish next to it, and maintains its position. This allows the entire group to swim as a unit, even though the school has no leader to command it.

When underwater light is poor and the fish cannot see, the schools tend to break up, with fish swimming every which way. Fish also have organs that sense the motions of other fish. Their *lateral line*, which runs from head to tail, is a chain of nerves that detects vibrations in the water. Thus fish can respond to the motion of other fish nearby and maintain their place in the school.

No one knows why some fish travel in schools and others do not. Usually the fish are of the same species and size. But traveling as a group does not give them any protection from predators; in fact, a school presents a better target for an attacker than a solitary fish that could easily slip away among the weeds. Certain aggressive fish, such as barracuda, travel in schools, which makes them very dangerous to an unwary swimmer or the fish they prey upon. Schools are not "families" of fish that swim together for breeding purposes; groups of fish that are either all-male or all-female will still swim in schools. Perhaps someday the mystery of fish schooling will be solved, as more information is gathered and analyzed.

SPOTFINNED TURKEY FISH

STONEFISH

PORCUPINE FISH   FOUR-SADDLE PUFFER

FISH OF THE REEFS

Most fish tend to take on, to a certain degree, the coloration of their natural surroundings.

Why are they brightly colored?

The fish inhabiting the shallow reefs in the warm southern seas are colored with all the brilliant tints of the rainbow.

These reefs are great jagged cliffs of coral rock that have been built up over millions of years by the skeletons of tiny sea animals called corals. The rock of the reefs varies in color from yellow to pink to orange to deep red. Most of the little fish that swim in and out among the reefs are just as gaily colored.

Not only are these fish of the tropic seas clothed in bright colors, but they take on some of the strangest forms of all the creatures of the deep. Some look like seaweed, and even like pieces of coral.

The *clownfish* gets its name because its body is colored like the face of a circus clown. It has a curious method of defending himself.

There is a poisonous plant-like animal living among the reefs called the sea anemone. When a small fish ventures too close to the tentacles of this "living flower," it is quickly stung to death and eaten. For some strange reason the anemone makes an exception of the funny little clownfish that swims in and out through the deadly tentacles in complete safety. When the clownfish is in danger, it dashes in among the anemone's tentacles where the other fish

CLOWN-BUTTERFLY

SPOTTED TRIGGERFISH

COWFISH

SEAMOTH

QUEEN ANGEL FISH

IMPERIAL ANGELFISH

HUMU HUMU
TRIGGERFISH

UNDULATE TRIGGERFISH

are afraid to follow. It even builds its nest where the anemone can protect it.

The *humuhumu-nukunuku-a-puaa*, also known by the less musical name of triggerfish, is a native of the South Pacific. It wears a brown mask over its eyes, like a bank robber, and its body looks like the head of a fish that has no body. Triggerfish make a grunting sound when they are taken from the water.

The *puffer* is a fish that can blow itself up like a balloon. When it is pulled from the water, it quickly swallows large amounts of air and water which cause it to expand to about three times its normal size. If it is thrown back, it floats upside down for several minutes until it expels the air and water from its body and returns to a normal swimming size.

Some puffers contain a deadly poison, called tetrodotoxin, which is used in preparing certain medicines. Yet in spite of this fact, they are prized as food fish in Japan. In order to cook these fish in restaurants, a Japanese must graduate from a puffer-cooking school. If the puffer is not properly cooked, the chances are better than even that the person who eats it will die.

The *sea moth* is a South Pacific fish that looks almost exactly like what its name implies — a beautifully colored moth. These little fellows are so rare that scientists know very little about them, not even enough to place them in an exact classification among the fish of the reefs.

SOUTHERN PUFFER BEFORE PUFFING

The *cowfish*, or trunkfish, not only has a pair of horns on its head, like a cow, but also lives encased in a hard shell like a turtle, with only its fins, eyes, jaws, and tail sticking out. The cowfish, considered a delicious food by South Sea islanders, is served cooked in its own shell.

The *porcupine fish* is equipped with the same kind of protection against its enemies as the animal of the same name that lives in our American forests. When in danger, it fills itself up with water and becomes a hard round ball covered with prickly spines. A big fish would have to be very hungry to swallow a porcupine fish when in this defensive condition.

The *stonefish* is a hideous fellow that lives in the shallow reefs and looks like a piece of coral. Moreover, it is as poisonous as a rattlesnake. The stonefish lies on the bottom, and if it is

SOUTHERN PUFFER PUFFED UP

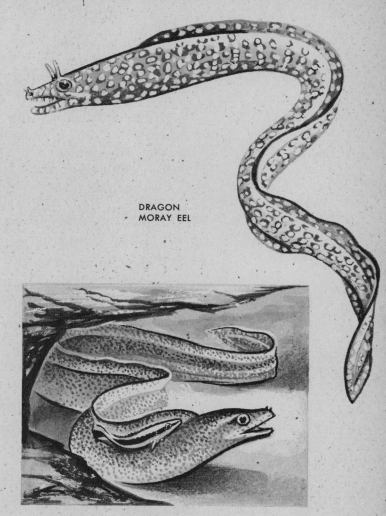

DRAGON MORAY EEL

The RAINBOW WRASSE is one of the "cleaners," shown here cleaning the parasites of a MORAY EEL. Needless to say, the Moray could easily swallow the little helper, but never would.

stepped on by a careless swimmer, its glands exude a venom that is deadly. Some people who have had the bad luck to step on a stonefish have died in less than two hours.

The *turkey fish* is a first cousin of the stonefish. It too is poisonous, but instead of looking like a piece of rock, it resembles the spread-out tail of a tom turkey.

The *moray eel* is the most evil and vicious looking of all the creatures of the reef. It sometimes grows to lengths of ten feet, and makes its home in narrow, underwater coral caves. As a rule, the moray stays in its cave during the day, sometimes with only its head sticking out, and emerges to forage for food at night.

The most brilliantly colored of the morays is the *dragon moray* found in Hawaiian waters. It has horns on its head, and its red and blue body is spotted with white dots. When the dragon moray moves through the clear tropical water, this strangely colored fish resembles a legendary sea monster.

Certain small fish, called "cleaners," remove and eat the parasites that collect on the moray's skin. Although the moray could gobble up these little cleaners in one gulp, it seems to be grateful for their sanitary service and allows them to work without harm, while the moray goes about his business.

Unusual Fish of the Sea

The incredible variety in the forms of fish species is one of the remarkable achievements of nature. It would take many months to become familiar with all of them, but here are a few of the most unusual ones.

How many different forms do fish take?

The *seahorse* gets its name because its head, neck and torso look very much like those of a thoroughbred horse. Actually, the creature looks like a finely carved knight in a chess set. It swims upright in the water, swaying from side to side. Sometimes it winds its tail around a rock or a piece of seaweed and

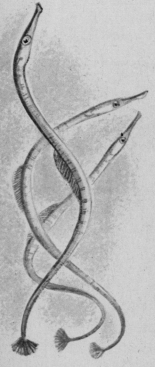

The PIPEFISH (above) and the SEAHORSE (at right) belong to the same order of fish. In spite of their different looks, they have many things in common. One of their common traits is the fact that the male, not the female, carries the young in a brood pouch.

SARGASSUM FISH

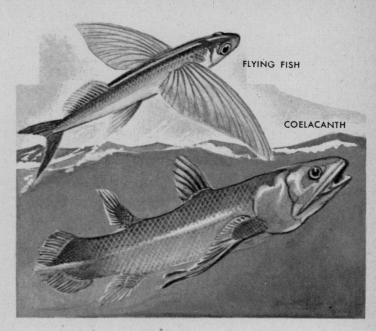

FLYING FISH

COELACANTH

HEAD OF A PIRANHA

The OCEAN SUNFISH (above) is a relative of the PORCUPINE FISH not of the PIGMY SUN-FISH (below), which is a freshwater fish.

remains almost motionless. Then, when some small fish swims innocently by, the seahorse dines on it.

One of the oddest things about the seahorse is that the father, not the mother, gives birth to the babies. The mother deposits her eggs in the father's brood pouch and then goes on her care-free way. When the eggs are hatched, the baby seahorses emerge from their father's body and swim off on their own.

There are about fifty different kinds of seahorses in the oceans of the world. They range in size from one inch to about fourteen inches high, and are brightly colored in shades of red, blue, and ivory.

The *leafy seadragon* is one of the rarest fishes in the whole great world of the sea. No more than half a dozen have ever been found. This odd creature is a distant cousin of the seahorse, and is about a foot long.

MUDSKIPPER

Its body is covered with a leafy growth that streams out in all directions like the fronds of the seaweed among which it makes its home. They render it indistinguishable from the seaweed itself.

The *sargassum fish* is one of nature's most perfect examples of protective coloration. It lives in the Sargassum Sea, a vast area of floating seaweed in the Atlantic just south of the Bermuda Islands. It is the same brown mottled color as the sargassum weed, and its long, lacy fins wave about in the water, just as the seaweed branches do.

The sargassum fish hovers quietly under a clump of weeds until another fish comes poking among the plants in search of something to eat. When it gets close enough to the sargassum fish's jaws, it quickly gets eaten up instead of finding a meal itself. The sargassum fish can eat other fish that are as big as it is by using its hand-like fins to stuff large mouthfuls down its throat.

In the warm waters of the South Atlantic, off West Africa, lives a peculiar fish called the *mudskipper*. Not only can it walk on land, but it even climbs trees in pursuit of insects.

The mudskipper is a throwback to the first fish that crawled out of the sea and developed into land animals so many millions of years ago. Its pectoral fins are attached to very strong leg-like appendages. When it leaves the water, it uses these fins to crawl, like a lizard.

Mudskippers can breathe air as well as water; sometimes they stay on land for long periods of time. They dig burrows in the mud of the swampy shore; and when danger approaches, they may either retreat to these holes or waddle over the mud to the safety of the sea (see illustration, pp. 14-15).

The mudskipper is only one of several species of lung-fish that are at home out of the water.

The *archerfish,* a native of Asiatic waters, kills airborne insects by shooting them down with pellets of water that it ejects from its mouth. Some archerfish fire only single shots at a time. Others shoot with the rapidity of a machine gun. If the archerfish hap-

The ARCHER, unlike most fish, has excellent vision and can hit an insect several feet away.

pens to miss its target on the first try, it quickly corrects its aim, and almost always makes a hit with the second attempt.

Since light rays are bent when they enter the water, scientists have been amazed that the archerfish can be so accurate when aiming at flying creatures above the surface. But the archers have developed the apparatus to solve this problem, and seldom fail to bring down their game.

The *ocean sunfish* looks like a gigantic fish head that has lost the rest of its body. A large one may weigh more than a ton. Its favorite food item is jellyfish. When it finds a large jellyfish, it first nibbles off the streaming tentacles, and finally bites into chunks of the jelly.

The ocean sunfish is one of nature's prize egg-layers. A single female will lay more than 300,000,000 eggs. Most of them are eaten by other fish, and only a few survive to grow up.

The *flying fish* does not really fly — that is, it does not flap its long wing-like fins as a bird does. Instead, by rushing rapidly through the water, it bursts through the surface and glides into the air like a coasting airplane for as much as 600 feet before it drops back into the ocean.

If you ever happen to be standing on the bow of a boat moving through tropical waters, you can see hundreds of flying fish spring out of the water ahead of the ship and skip over the waves in every direction, splashing up sprays of water as they go (see illustration, title page).

The *coelacanth*. One day in 1938, a man fishing off the African coast of the Indian Ocean found a strange-looking fish in his net. It was five feet long, and weighed about 125 pounds. The fisherman had never seen anything like it, and so he sent it to a museum.

If the fisherman had found a dinosaur roaming wild in the hills, he would not have attracted more attention in the scientific world. The curious fish was a *coelacanth* (pronounced seal-a-canth), a species that scientists thought had become extinct nearly one hundred million years ago! Coelacanths had long been known in fossil form, but no one had ever expected to see one alive.

In the years that followed the first discovery of a live coelacanth, several other of these "living fossils" have been captured. Scientists believe that they, like the lung fish, were among the ancestors of present-day amphibians, reptiles, birds, and mammals.

The *remora* is the hitchhiker of the ocean. By means of a flat sucking disk on the top of its head, it attaches itself to the undersides of sharks and other large fish, which carry the remora along with them.

Unlike lampreys, the remora does not suck blood from its host. It just goes along for the ride — and also for free meals. When the shark eats, fragments of its food float in the water around it. The remora then releases its hold and feeds on these scraps.

The *electric eel,* found in the inland rivers of South America, is one of the most spectacular of all fish. It grows to a length of six feet, and is capable of shooting an electrical discharge of 600 volts, which is about five times the shock you would get if you stuck your finger into an electrical outlet in your home. It is not surprising that it has no enemies. No other water creatures dare come within reach of it.

The eel uses its electric battery to both locate and kill its prey. Although the eel has eyes when it is young, it becomes blind as it grows to maturity. Its radiation of electric impulses enables it to locate food, working on much the same principle as radar. When it locates its prey, it gives the unhappy fish a jolt that knocks it out. The eel then proceeds to eat it leisurely.

The essential organs of the eel's body are contained in about one fifth of its length. The other four-fifths of its body comprise its powerful electrical battery, consisting of layers of tissue one behind another similar to battery plates.

SEA COLANDER

The *piranha,* also a native of South American rivers, is the most vicious of all the world's fish. It is only ten to twelve inches long, but its teeth are so sharp and its jaws so strong that it can chop out a piece of a man, an alligator, or a deer as neatly as the sharpest razor. The piranha, with one bite, can take off a man's finger.

Piranhas travel in schools of several hundred. Normally, their diet consists of other small fish. But if a large animal happens to be in the water near a school of pirhanas, they devour it instantly. In one recorded instance, a *capybara,* a large South American animal weighing one hundred pounds, was eaten down to a bare skeleton by a school of piranhas in less than a minute. On rare, unlucky occasions, people have suffered the same fate.

Piranhas are valued by South American natives as food fish. But even out of the water they are dangerous. After being caught and put in a boat, and apparently dead, they have been known to snap their jaws and bite off the finger of an unwary fisherman.

The *giant oarfish,* or ribbon-fish, usually found in southern waters, has given rise to many tales of mysterious sea serpents. It may grow to a length of thirty feet or more, yet its long body may be only twelve inches deep and no more than two inches thick.

As it swims along close to the surface, it undulates like a snake. Science has been unable to observe much about the habits of this unusual fish because it is rarely seen or captured.

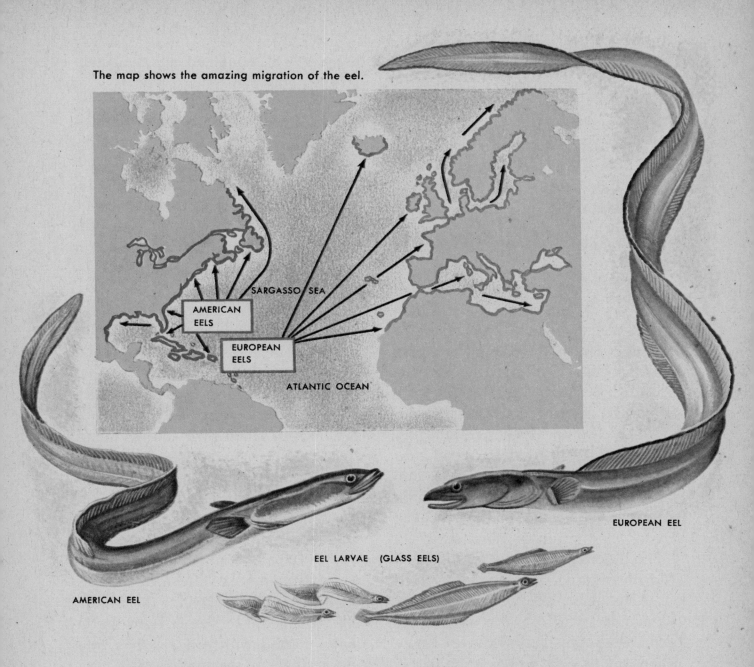

The map shows the amazing migration of the eel.

SARGASSO SEA

AMERICAN EELS

EUROPEAN EELS

ATLANTIC OCEAN

EUROPEAN EEL

EEL LARVAE (GLASS EELS)

AMERICAN EEL

Fish on the Go

THE MYSTERIOUS MIGRATION OF THE EEL

The life story of the eel — and of its mysterious migration from its birthplace in the South Atlantic Ocean to the inland rivers and lakes of Europe and North America — is one of the most fascinating in all the annals of the sea.

How does the eel know where to go?

Eels have been prized as table delicacies since the days of the early Greeks and Romans. But their origin remained a mystery; no eel eggs or larvae were ever seen.

Greek and Roman naturalists had a great many theories about where the eels came from. Some thought that they grew from earthworms, or from horse hairs that had fallen into the water. It was not until the early part of this century that the mystery of the eel was solved. And when it was, the facts proved to be almost as unbelievable as ancient fantasies.

We now know that all North American and European eels are born in the Sargasso Sea, the great jungle of matted seaweed in the Atlantic, south of Bermuda. The mother eel lays from ten million to fifteen million eggs and the father eel fertilizes them. Then both parents die. Shortly thereafter, the curious life cycle of the newborn eels begins.

Where are eels born?

The tiny round eggs hatch, and after a few months the baby eels develop into flat, glassy, transparent creatures about an inch or two long. These are called *leptocephali,* meaning "thin heads."

The little leptocephali then begin to swim northward. And now another curious thing takes place. In some mysterious manner, which science has not yet been able to explain, the little eels know which way to swim to reach the native waters of their parents. Both American eels and European eels are born in the same part of the Sargasso Sea. Yet the American eels turn westward from the Sargasso Sea, and the European eels turn toward the east. No one has ever caught an American eel in European rivers, nor a European eel in America.

The life cycles of both kinds of eels are identical, except that it takes a European eel three years to make its journey to the mainland, and the American eel only one.

When the babies reach the coastlines, they are fully developed eels, although still only about three inches in length. At this stage, they are called *elvers.* Now the males stay in the mouths of the rivers and in the sea near the shore; the females swim inland up the rivers.

What are elvers?

Sometimes the female eels swim for hundreds of miles, until they come to rest at last in ponds and lakes and creeks or the quiet headwaters of rivers. They make their way over dams and waterfalls, and often go through sewers and pipelines to reach their journey's end. Eels have been found in inland ponds that have neither an inlet nor an outlet. This leads us to believe that they wriggle overland through swamps and wet grass to reach such destinations.

The female eels remain in inland waters from seven to fifteen years, while the males patiently wait for them in the sea water close to shore. Then the females start downstream on their long journey back to the Sargasso Sea.

When they reach the ocean waters, they are joined once again by the males. And together they swim the thousands of miles back to the place where they were born.

In the tangled weeds of the Sargasso Sea, they mate, and the female lays her eggs. They never go back to the mainland again, but die as their parents did. Their offspring take up the amazing cycle of eel life.

Eight-foot-long electric eel can give a man a deadly shock.

Electric eels are found in the rivers of South America, where they use their electricity to stun their prey and ward off attackers. Just how they generate and store so much electricity is not fully understood. But three-fourths of the eel's body — its entire tail — is devoted to organs of an electrical nature. The eel's heart, lungs, and other body organs are crammed into the small front section of the fish.

The eel's jellylike electric organs consist of thousands of waferlike cells, or "batteries," each of which generates one-tenth of a volt. These are stacked in columns of six thousand cells linked by nerves which make the electrical connections from cell to cell. The cells in each column are "wired" in such a way that their voltages add up to a maximum of six hundred volts. An electric eel has 140 of these "storage batteries."

When the eel is touched, it may discharge its batteries by reflex action. Pulses of electric current flow from the eel's head through the water to its tail, where the circuit is completed. The minerals dissolved in a river make river water a fairly good conductor of electricity. A fish or person swimming in the path of the electric current is likely to get a terrific jolt. In one second the eel may deliver dozens of electric shocks, after which its "batteries" are exhausted. It must then rest for five minutes until its electric organs are recharged.

Are electric eels dangerous? Certain catfish, rays, and eels have organs that can generate electricity. Of all these electric fishes, the electric eel is the most dangerous. A fully grown eight-foot-long electric eel can deliver a shock so powerful that it can kill a man. An electric eel usually delivers a shock of about 250 volts (twice the voltage of ordinary house current), but sometimes it gives off a 600-volt jolt. A baby electric eel generates the same voltage as an adult eel, but it can't deliver as much current.

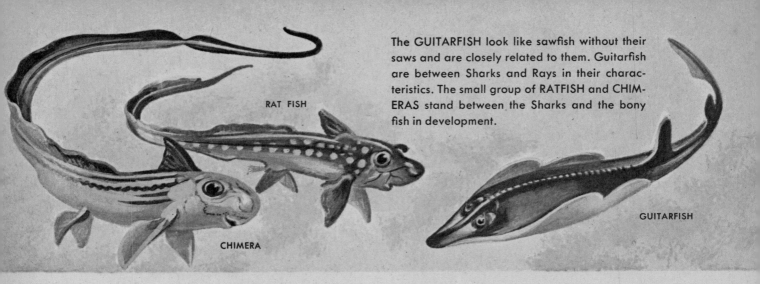

RAT FISH

The GUITARFISH look like sawfish without their saws and are closely related to them. Guitarfish are between Sharks and Rays in their characteristics. The small group of RATFISH and CHIMERAS stand between the Sharks and the bony fish in development.

CHIMERA

GUITARFISH

SOME MORE INTERESTING FISH

The members of the MACKEREL group all have distinctly forked tails. They travel in schools and most of them have a high commercial value as game and foodfish. The SMELT, averaging about 7 or 8 ounces, are smaller relatives of the Salmon. The HOGSUCKER is a typical representative of the Suckergroup, widely distributed in American fresh waters. The SNOOK is an excellent game and foodfish related to the Seabass; it inhabits tropical seas. The MUSKELUNGE, a freshwater fish, forms, with Pike and Pickerel, a group of fine game and foodfish. The RAINBOW DARTER is a nicely colored fish about 3 inches long, inhabiting lakes and creeks; it is a member of the Perch family. The male of the RED BELLIED DACE is brightly colored and grows to about 5 inches in length. It belongs to the Minnow family. The largest representative of the Minnow family is the CARP, a valuable foodfish, introduced from Europe to the United States. The Goldfish also belongs to the Carp family. The SEA RAVEN is an ugly fish about 20 to 25 inches; it inhabits the cooler waters of the world and is a member of the Sculpin family, which is of no value to man. The SWORDFISH is a good gamefish fighter and a tasty foodfish. It grows up to 15 feet in length and dwells in the warmer regions of the Atlantic and Pacific. The RED SNAPPER, a member of the tropical Snapper group, is a good foodfish. The DOLPHIN, not to be confused with the sea mammal of the same name, are extremely fast swimmers, often observed on the surface of the tropical waters.

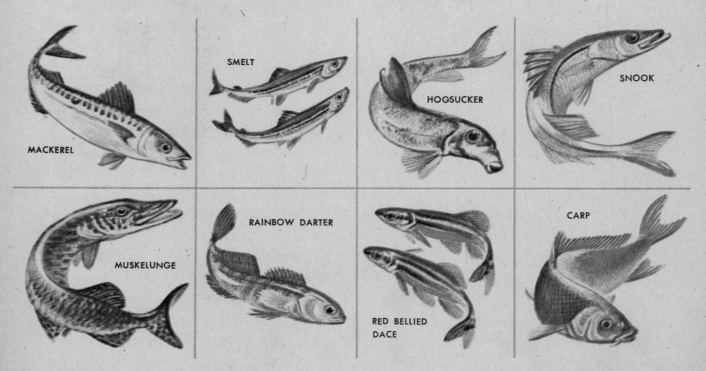

SMELT

HOGSUCKER

SNOOK

MACKEREL

RAINBOW DARTER

CARP

MUSKELUNGE

RED BELLIED DACE

SEA RAVEN

SWORDFISH

RED SNAPPER

DOLPHIN

The KISSING GOURAMI and the SIAMESE FIGHTING FISH are both members of the same family of small tropical fresh-water fish of Africa and South East Asia. In parts of Asia contests are held, in which the male of the Fighting Fish fight each other. Observers place bets on the outcome.

KISSING GOURAMI

SIAMESE FIGHTING FISH

WHALE

DOLPHIN

PORPOISE

DUGONG

MAMMALS THAT LOOK LIKE FISH

WHALES, DOLPHINS, PORPOISES and DUGONGS are the descendants of sea creatures that once lived on the land, but for some unknown reason, returned to the sea millions of years ago. They are streamlined like fish, and swim through the water just as effortlessly as a fish does. What was once their forelegs, has been modified into flippers with which they steer themselves; their hindlegs have disappeared entirely. Although they look like fish, they are air breathing mammals that bear their young live and suckle them on the mother's milk. These fish are also warm blooded mammals that have special protective layers of fat to prevent them from losing too much temperature in the cold waters.

RED SALMON

WHITEFISH

Related to the Salmon, but with larger scales, is the WHITEFISH family, the most important food-fish of our northern inland waters.

ATLANTIC SALMON

THE LONG JOURNEY OF THE SALMON

Like the eel, the salmon is also a migratory fish, spending part of its life in fresh-water streams and the other part in the sea. But nature, in her wonderfully mysterious way, has arranged the salmon's life cycle exactly opposite to that of the eel's.

Why does this fresh-water fish go to sea?

The salmon is born inland, in the headwaters of rivers. Later it goes down the rivers, swims far out to sea to spend the greater part of its life span, and then returns to its native river where it spawns and finally dies.

The salmon's life story begins when the female digs a trench in the sandy bottom of a crystal clear mountain stream. Here she lays her eggs. After the male salmon fertilizes the eggs, the female fills in the trench with sweeping strokes of her strong tail. Then both the parent fish die. Their mission in life has been accomplished.

After about 2½ months the young *alevins,* as they are called, burst forth from the eggs. For a while they feed on a yolk sac which they carry with them. Then they live happily for several years in the waters where they were born. During this period they are called *fry,* but when they begin their long journeys, they are known as *smolts.*

An instinctive urge tells them that it is time to go down the river and out to sea. So down the rivers they go. Millions of them congregate at the mouths of rivers in the brackish waters emptying into the ocean. Then all together, in a great mass migration, they set out for the unknown reaches of the sea.

No one knows exactly where they go,
or how far out to sea they venture. We do know that they stay in the ocean for about five or six years. Then a strange homing urge comes upon them, and they return to the rivers of their birth.

How long do they stay at sea?

Getting back is a difficult job. They have to breast the swift, raging currents of mountain streams. They leap up over dams and waterfalls.

Amazingly enough, the salmon's in-stinct usually takes it back to the very river where it was born, even though it has spent many years in the deep waters of the sea. Some scientists believe it is able to do so by means of its sense of smell.

One kind of salmon does not migrate. They are called land-locked salmon. They live in ponds and lakes that have no outlet to the sea, mostly in Canada and the State of Maine. Thus, the land-locked salmon spends all of its life in fresh water.

Keeping Fish as Pets

No fish can be a true pet, in the sense that a dog or a cat is able to give us affection and companionship. But keeping tropical fish in a home aquarium can be an interesting and entertaining hobby. The beautiful coloring and conformation of these little creatures make them a constant pleasure to watch as they swim among the waterplants in the tank.

A wide selection of tropical fish can be purchased at almost any pet shop or variety store, and at very little cost. Of course, certain rare specimens imported from abroad are very expensive, but they are only acquired by dedicated fish fanciers. The aquarium in which you keep your fish will vary in price according to its size. The size will be determined by the

What kind of specimens can you buy?

number of fish you have.

A good rule of thumb in choosing a tank is to allow one gallon of water for every two fish. In this way they will be assured of an ample oxygen supply. Thus, if you decide to start with six fish, your tank should hold at least three gallons of water.

You should also remember that the water you use must be soft. A fish's skin is protected by a layer of mucous over its scales. Hard water destroys this coating and kills the fish. Therefore, if the tap water in your community is hard, use rain water, or water from a nearby pond.

You should also keep water plants in the tank. These plants give off oxygen and absorb the gases that are harmful to the fish, thus

What do water plants do?

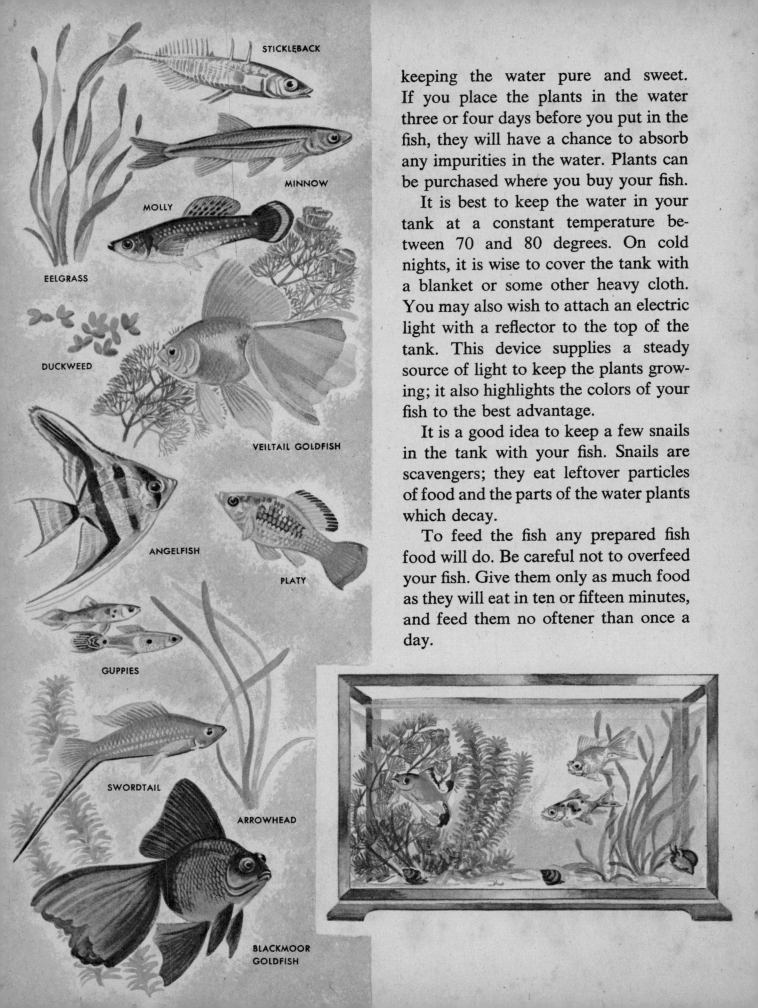

STICKLEBACK

MINNOW

MOLLY

EELGRASS

DUCKWEED

VEILTAIL GOLDFISH

ANGELFISH

PLATY

GUPPIES

SWORDTAIL

ARROWHEAD

BLACKMOOR
GOLDFISH

keeping the water pure and sweet. If you place the plants in the water three or four days before you put in the fish, they will have a chance to absorb any impurities in the water. Plants can be purchased where you buy your fish.

It is best to keep the water in your tank at a constant temperature between 70 and 80 degrees. On cold nights, it is wise to cover the tank with a blanket or some other heavy cloth. You may also wish to attach an electric light with a reflector to the top of the tank. This device supplies a steady source of light to keep the plants growing; it also highlights the colors of your fish to the best advantage.

It is a good idea to keep a few snails in the tank with your fish. Snails are scavengers; they eat leftover particles of food and the parts of the water plants which decay.

To feed the fish any prepared fish food will do. Be careful not to overfeed your fish. Give them only as much food as they will eat in ten or fifteen minutes, and feed them no oftener than once a day.